UNDERSTANDING
BUDDHISM

Origins • Beliefs • Practices
Holy Texts • Sacred Places

UNDERSTANDING
BUDDHISM

Origins • Beliefs • Practices
Holy Texts • Sacred Places

Malcolm David Eckel

DUNCAN BAIRD PUBLISHERS

LONDON

Understanding Buddhism
Malcolm David Eckel

First published in the United Kingdom and Ireland in 2003 by
Duncan Baird Publishers Ltd
Sixth Floor
Castle House
75–76 Wells Street
London W1T 3QH

Conceived, created and designed by Duncan Baird Publishers

Project Editor: Christopher Westhorp
Senior Editor: Diana Loxley
Design: Cobalt id
Picture Researcher: Julia Ruxton

British Library Cataloguing-in-Publication Data:
A CIP record for this book is available from the British Library

ISBN: 1-904292-11-9

10 9 8 7 6 5 4 3 2

Typeset in Garamond Three
Colour reproduction by Scanhouse, Malaysia
Printed and bound in Singapore by Imago

NOTES
The abbreviations BCE and CE are used throughout this book:
BCE Before the Common Era (the equivalent of BC)
CE Common Era (the equivalent of AD)

Page 2: The Mahabodhi Temple at Bodh Gaya, India, marking the site
where the Buddha, Siddhartha Gautama, achieved his awakening.

Dedication
In memory of William Neville Smith (1947–2001)
a talented scholar of Buddhism who chose another path

CONTENTS

INTRODUCTION

Buddhism takes its name from Siddhartha Gautama, who was revered by his disciples as the Buddha, or "Awakened One." In the course of only a few centuries, his teaching spread across the Indian subcontinent and into many other parts of Asia. Although it later almost died out as a living religion in the land of its origin, Buddhism has had a profound impact on religious life and cultural development outside India, from Afghanistan in the west to China, Korea, and Japan in the east, and through southeast Asia from Myanmar (Burma) as far as the Indonesian islands of Java and Bali. Today, Buddhism is also a vibrant part of the religious landscape of Europe and North America.

According to a widely accepted scholarly chronology, Siddhartha Gautama was born in 566BCE and died aged eighty in 486BCE. Buddhist tradition reports that he was born in what is now southern Nepal to royal parents. His birth was associated with a series of omens that portended the significance of his career. According to one account of the Buddha's life, when the future Buddha was conceived, his mother, Queen Maya, dreamt that a white elephant painlessly entered her side. When the time came for the young Siddhartha to be born, he sprang from his mother's side, took seven steps, and said:

A 19th-century Burmese manuscript painting depicts Siddhartha Gautama meditating while being assailed by the forces of the demon king Mara (see pp.8–9).

"I have been born to achieve awakening (*bodhi*) for the good of the world: this is my last birth."

Siddhartha's father asked the court sages to interpret these marvels. The sages saw wheels on the child's hands and feet, and predicted that he would grow up to be a *Chakravartin* ("Wheel-Turner")—either a mighty conquering king or a great religious teacher.

Siddhartha was raised in his father's palace, was married, and had a son. In his early thirties, he became curious about life outside the palace and asked to go beyond its walls. In a garden he saw three sights that brought home the reality of human suffering: an old man, a sick man, and a corpse. On another occasion, he saw a fourth sight—a wandering ascetic (*shramana*)—and vowed that he would follow the ascetic's example and seek release from the world of suffering. His father tried to restrain him, but Siddhartha Gautama assumed the life of a wanderer. This event, known as the Pravrajya ("Going Forth"), is reenacted in Buddhist communities whenever anyone decides to take up the life of a monk or a nun.

The earliest stages of Siddhartha's withdrawal were marked by severe fasting and self-denial—so much so that he almost died. Convinced that this route to salvation was unproductive, he accepted food from a young woman and began to follow what is known in Buddhist tradition as the "Middle Way," a mode of discipline that avoids the extremes of self-indulgence and self-denial.

Siddhartha's wanderings eventually brought him to the foot of the Bodhi Tree or the "Tree of Awakening." He seated himself beneath it in a last attempt to win freedom from death and rebirth. He was assailed by the evil god Mara, who sent his daughters to seduce him and his sons to frighten him away. But Siddhartha withstood

Mara's onslaught and, during one final night of meditation, became enlightened about the Dharma ("truth" or "law") of human existence. With this he could properly be called a *buddha* ("awakened one").

After his awakening, the Buddha walked to a deer park at Sarnath, near Varanasi, where he met five of his former companions. He taught them a sermon, or discourse (*sutra*), known as the "First Turning of the Wheel of the Dharma [Law]." The story of Buddhism as an organized religious tradition begins with the serene and newly wise teacher conveying the results of his awakening to a handful of companions, who formed the nucleus of the Buddhist *samgha* ("community"). For the remaining forty-five years of his life, the Buddha wandered the roads of northern India, preaching the Dharma and expanding the boundaries of the community. Finally, in the town of Kushinagari, he delivered a closing discourse to his disciples, lay down between two trees, and died. In Buddhist terms, he achieved his "final *nirvana*" (perfect enlightenment; *parinirvana*), never to be reborn.

The Buddhist tradition evolved in many complex ways after the death of the Buddha, but it has retained the same practical focus. The Buddha was not considered to be God or a supernatural being, but a man who had found the answer to the deepest dilemmas of human life and had made that answer available to others. For millions of people worldwide, Buddhism conveys a sense of the sacred and a sense of social and cultural cohesion without reliance on the concept of a creator God.

About a century after the Buddha's death, the first divisions arose in the Buddhist community. Eighteen rival "schools" (*nikaya*s) emerged, of which only Theravada, the dominant tradition of present-day southeast Asia, survives. In the third century BCE, the patronage of the Indian emperor Ashoka (see p.16) brought Buddhism to Sri Lanka, whence it traveled to southeast Asia, including Indonesia. In the second century CE, monks took Buddhism along the Silk Road to China, from where it passed to Korea and thence to Japan. Tibetan Buddhism took root in the seventh century CE and today is one of the most recognizable Buddhist cultures.

The success of Buddhism in northern and eastern Asia was enhanced by the emergence of the Mahayana, or "Great Vehicle," movement in India, around the beginning of the Common Era. The Mahayana brought with it a new body of scriptures, a new emphasis on the importance of laypeople, and a new concept—the Buddha. Tantric Buddhism, an offshoot of Mahayana, appeared in the seventh century CE. With its emphasis on symbolism and ritual and its vision of *buddha*s as "wrathful" deities,

Tantra is one of the most challenging varieties of Buddhism. Schools of Tantric Buddhism are found in China, Japan, Tibet, and Nepal.

The institutional and intellectual expansion of Buddhism was fostered by several remarkable personalities, beginning with the Buddha's early followers. Both Mahayana and Theravada produced a series of scholar-monks who gave intellectual shape to the monastic tradition of southeast Asia. Buddhism has also given rise to religious and social reformers such as Shinran and Nichiren in Japan, and has a tradition of political engagement, from the emperor Ashoka to the two recent Buddhist recipients of the Nobel Peace Prize, the fourteenth Dalai Lama and Myanmar's Aung San Suu Kyi.

There have also, of course, been generations of ordinary Buddhists whose stories have not been preserved but who have given meaning to their lives through the simple gestures of Buddhist worship: by observing the "Five Precepts" (see pp.59–60); by offering food to monks; by celebrating rites of passage; by participating in celebrations of the Buddha's birthday or of Buddhist "saints"; or by going on a pilgrimage. All of these aspects of Buddhist practice seem to express, in one form or another, the same fundamental impulse—to find serenity in a world of suffering and change.

CHAPTER ONE

ORIGINS AND HISTORICAL DEVELOPMENT

The history of Buddhism as a distinct religious tradition began with the life of the Buddha, Siddhartha Gautama, also known as Shakyamuni or "the Sage of the Shakya Clan," who was born in India near the end of the sixth century BCE.

Inspired by the Buddha's teaching, Buddhism spread from India to Sri Lanka, and from there to much of southeast Asia. In the first or second century of the Common Era, it was transported north across the Silk Road to China. From China it was taken to Korea, Japan, and Vietnam. During the seventh century, Buddhist teachers moved north across the Himalayas and carried the faith to Tibet. In the modern period, Buddhism has spread far beyond its home in India to become a vital part of world civilization.

LEFT: A detail (ca. 1800) from the Vessantara Jataka—*one of the most popular of the* Jataka *tales (see p.14)—showing Prince Vessantara, a previous incarnation of the Buddha.*

From a Buddhist point of view, the story of the Buddhist tradition does not begin in the sixth century BCE with the birth of Siddhartha Gautama, but in the distant past, with the stories of his previous lives as a *bodhisattva* or "future buddha." According to the doctrine of rebirth (*samsara*), a person's life is the result of a long series of actions (*karma*) accumulated over a process of many lifetimes, and Siddhartha Gautama was no exception. A body of traditional texts known as the *Jataka* ("Birth") tales describes how he received teaching from previous *buddha*s, exhibited many of the moral virtues of the Buddhist tradition, and prepared for his final awakening.

While Buddhists view the career of Siddhartha Gautama as the result of a long process of preparation, they also see it as the beginning of a new historical process, in which others have attempted to follow his example and experience his awakening for themselves.

After the Buddha's death or "final *nirvana*" (*parinirvana*), a group of lay disciples, following his instructions, cremated his body, distributed his ashes as relics, and enshrined them in funerary mounds, or *stupa*s. The veneration of these remains provided the model for the tradition of Buddhist worship, which came to be directed not only at relics but also at other objects, images, and sites sanctified through their association with events in the Buddha's life. In Buddhist tradition, these constitute the Buddha's "Form Body," while his teaching is known as his "Dharma Body." In the two types of "body" (often understood differently in different parts of the Buddhist world), the Buddha continues to be a presence in the wider Buddhist community.

Most of the evidence for the early history of the Buddhist community, the *samgha*, comes from texts written five centuries or more after the Buddha's death. It is therefore difficult to establish for certain how the *samgha* grew from a small band of disciples around a single charismatic leader to become a major force in India and beyond. However, Buddhist tradition records several stages of institutional development that made it possible for the religion to play an important role in the growth of Asian civilization.

A short time after the Buddha's death in 486BCE, a "First Buddhist Council" is said to have been held in the city of Rajagrha. In one account, the Buddha's disciple Kashyapa was traveling with a group of monks when he heard that his master had died. One monk openly rejoiced, saying that his death freed them from the constraints of monastic rules. Fearing a breakdown in discipline, Kashyapa proposed the calling of a council to restate the Buddha's teaching and monastic regulations and set down a common body of doctrine and practice to guide the Buddhist community. The council produced what was to become the nucleus of the Buddhist canon.

Another tradition tells of a second council, called about a century later in the city of Vaishali to discuss variations to the monastic code introduced under the pressure of the community's regional expansion. However, the issues were not fully resolved and gave rise to Buddhism's first big schism, between the Sthaviras ("Elders") and Mahasamghikas ("Great Community"). This was the start of the fragmentation of the *samgha* into the Eighteen Schools (*nikaya*s), and anticipated the eventual split between Hinayana ("Lesser Vehicle") Buddhism and Mahayana ("Greater Vehicle") Buddhism.

The expansion of the early Buddhist community owed much to royal patronage, both within India and beyond. The great Mauryan emperor Ashoka (268–239BCE), who ruled northern India from his capital at Pataliputra (modern Patna), made an explicit and public conversion to Buddhism. As part of his policy of "righteous conquest" (*dharmavijaya*), he promulgated Buddhist values throughout his kingdom and actively supported the spread of the religion beyond his frontiers. For example, his son Mahendra (Pali: Mahinda) is said to have gone to Sri Lanka at the head of a mission.

At this time it seems there were also Buddhist monks in the region of Afghanistan and central Asia, where they came into contact with Hellenic kingdoms established after Alexander the Great's invasion of India in 327–325 BCE. At least one Greek king, Menander (Pali: Milinda), is said to have converted to Buddhism.

The split between Hinayana and Mahayana Buddhism took place around the beginning of the Common Era, in circumstances that are still poorly understood. The Mahayana reform movement traced its history back to the Buddha himself. According to Mahayana texts, the Buddha held a special assembly at the Vulture Peak in Rajagrha and delivered a sermon known as "the Second Turning of the Wheel of the Dharma" to a select group of disciples. This teaching, it is said, remained hidden for a period and was then revealed to the rest of the Indian Buddhist community.

Whether the Mahayana emerged in one region of India or developed in several different centers is uncertain. But it is clear that its emphasis on the *bodhisattva* ideal incorporated the interests of lay Buddhists, both men and women, in a new way. A *bodhisattva* did not seek to renounce the world to attain *nirvana*, as in the traditional monastic ideal, but returned to the world out of compassion for ordinary humanity.

*One of the four carved gateways (*toranas*) to the Great Stupa
at Sanchi, which dates from the time of Ashoka and was much
embellished in later centuries.*

Tantric Buddhism—a movement that arose out of
Mahayana Buddhism in the sixth century—seemed to
challenge the most fundamental commitments of the
tradition. The term Tantra comes from the name of the
texts that convey its teachings, and is also known as the
Mantrayana ("Vehicle of Sacred Chants") and Vajrayana
("Vehicle of the Thunderbolt"). Tantric Buddhism
stresses ritual and symbolism, especially the *mandala* or
"sacred circle" (see pp.32–3), and promotes practices

aimed at achieving an immediate experience of "awakening." The radical quality of this awakening is most vividly expressed in Tantric art by the depiction of the Buddha as a "wrathful deity." A Tantric *siddha* or "saint" understands that there is no difference between peacefulness and anger, and that the awakening experience is present in even the most basic of human emotions.

For the first six or seven centuries CE, Buddhism was central to a great flowering of Indian culture, notably in the period of the Gupta dynasty (320–540CE) and the reign of King Harsha (606–646CE). Buddhist monasteries were sophisticated centers of learning, training monks in philosophy, religion, medicine, astronomy, and grammar. By the thirteenth century, however, the rise of Hindu devotionalism in India seems to have undermined the appeal of Buddhism to the common people, while centuries of Buddhist and Hindu interaction eroded the differences between the two traditions. Without strong support from India's kings and princes, Buddhist monasteries were vulnerable to persecution. When Muslim invaders destroyed the last major monasteries at the end of the thirteenth century, Buddhism's active influence on Indian culture effectively ended.

The history of Buddhism in southeast Asia goes back to Ashoka's missionaries in Sri Lanka. For a thousand years or more, the Buddhism of this region was an eclectic mix of traditions that mirrored the diversity of Indian Buddhism. From the eleventh century, when the influence of Indian monasteries began to wane, a number of Buddhist monks and kings in Myanmar and Thailand looked abroad for guidance. Following the example of Sri Lanka, they adopted the Theravada orthodoxy, and this branch of Buddhism predominates in Myanmar and Thailand to this day. In the nineteenth and twentieth centuries, southeast Asian Buddhists were confronted by European colonialism, but generations of reformers rose to the challenge and developed a distinctively "modern" form of Buddhism.

The religion came to Tibet in two waves, known as the "First" and "Second Diffusion of the Dharma." The first began in the seventh century CE, when the wives of the Tibetan king brought images of the Buddha to the capital, Lhasa. The first monastery was established at Samye in the late eighth century CE with the collaboration of the Indian scholar Shantarakshita, the Tibetan king Thrisong Detsen, and the Indian Tantric saint Padmasambhava. The history of Tibetan Buddhism is characterized by the elements that these three founders represent: monastic intellectual discipline; royal secular power; and Tantric ritual and meditation.

The "First Diffusion of the Dharma" in Tibet came to an end during a period of persecution that began in the reign of King Langdarma (838–842CE). Buddhism was reintroduced to Tibet at the end of the tenth century in what is known as the "Later Diffusion," and by the end of the eleventh century, the four main sects of Tibetan Buddhism had been clearly distinguished. One, the Nyingmapa, traced its origin back to Padmasambhava. The others—the Sakyapa, Kadampa, and Kargyupa—claimed to be rooted in the saints and scholars who came after the great persecution. From the Kadampa sect sprang the Gelukpa lineage that eventually produced the Dalai Lamas.

The title Dalai Lama (literally "Ocean Teacher," the first word presumably meaning "Ocean of Wisdom") was first given to the Tibetan monk Sonam Gyatso (1543–88CE) by the Mongol chief Altan Khan. However, Tibetan Buddhists consider Sonam Gyatso to be the third in a line of reincarnations that leads back to the monk Gendun Dup (1391–1475), who is therefore regarded as the true "first" Dalai Lama.

During the reign of the "Great Fifth" Dalai Lama, Ngawang Losang Gyatso (1617–82), the Dalai Lamas became the full secular and religious leaders of Tibet. Under their leadership, Tibetan Buddhists maintained their traditional way of life until the Chinese invasion of Tibet in 1950 forced Tenzin Gyatso, the fourteenth Dalai Lama, into exile. Since that time, he has been the focus of efforts to preserve Tibetan culture, both in Tibet and among communities of converts and exiles around the world.

Buddhism entered China in the first (or possibly second) century CE along the Silk Road. As in southeast Asia and Tibet, the religion's greatest initial challenge was how to express the richness and complexity of Indian Buddhism in an indigenous form. However, by the time of the Tang dynasty (618–907CE), Buddhism had become thoroughly acculturated and was playing an important role in Chinese civilization. This period saw the emergence of the classic Chinese Mahayana schools, including the meditation tradition of Chan (from Sanskrit *dhyana*, "meditation") and the philosophical schools of Tiantai and Huayan. Chinese Buddhism was also deeply influenced by the Mahayana tradition of celestial *buddha*s and *bodhisattva*s, especially Amitabha (Amituo Fo), Avalokiteshvara (Guanyin), and Maitreya (Mile Fo).

The Chinese variety of Buddhism was introduced to Korea in the fourth century CE and to Japan in the sixth century CE. Vietnam also came to adopt Chinese

Buddhist traditions, although the religion may originally have penetrated the region as early as the second century CE. A form of Chan Buddhism (Japanese: Zen), with its emphasis on meditation and the experience of "awakening," occurs in all three lands, as does a degree of devotion to celestial *buddha*s and *bodhisattva*s.

Scarcely known in the Western world (except to scholars) before ca. 1850, Buddhism had begun to spread actively there by 1900, due in part to an ex-US Army colonel, Henry S. Olcott (1832–1907), and a Russian mystic, Helena Blavatsky (1831–91). They took up the cause of reviving Theravada Buddhism in colonial Sri Lanka, and their Theosophical Society owed much to Buddhist precepts. The faith's profile was also raised by the World Parliament of Religions, held in Chicago in 1893, which was attended by many important Asian Buddhist figures.

By the mid-twentieth century, almost all of the major Buddhist schools and traditions had come to be represented in the West, both among immigrant communities and Western converts. In monasteries, temples, and meditation halls from Scotland to San Francisco, Buddhism has put down vigorous roots in environments quite different from that of the Ganges Basin, where it came into being.

Xuanzang's Visit to the Bodhi Tree

❝ The Master of the Law, when he came to worship the Bodhi tree and the figure of Tathagata at the time of his reaching perfect wisdom, made (*afterwards*) by (*the interposition of*) Maitreya Bodhisattva, gazed on these objects with the most sincere devotion, he cast himself down with his face to the ground in worship, and with much grief and many tears in his self-affliction, he sighed, and said: 'At the time when the Buddha perfected himself in wisdom, I know not in what condition I was, in the troublous world of birth and death; but now, in this latter time of image (*worship*), having come to this spot and reflecting on the depth and weight of the body of my evil deeds, I am grieved at heart, and my eyes are filled with tears.' ❞

From *The Life of Hiuen-tsiang*, translated by Samuel Beal. Kegan, Paul, Trench, Trübner & Co. Ltd.: London, 1911, p.105.

Commentary

The travel diary of the Chinese monk and scholar Xuanzang (596–664CE) provides one of the richest sources of information about Buddhism in India during its classical period (third to eighth century). Xuanzang traveled as a pilgrim across the Silk Road, through Afghanistan, where he admired the massive, gilded, rock-cut statues of the Buddha at Bamiyan, and over the Khyber Pass to northern India.

Xuanzang spent more than ten years in India, during which time he explored Buddhist sites as far apart as the mountains of Kashmir in the north and the Tamil-speaking lands of south India. Every place he turned seemed to present a story connected with an event in the Buddha's life, the life of a previous *buddha*, or the life of a famous Buddhist saint.

In Afghanistan, he visited the cave of the Buddha's shadow and had a vision of the Buddha's body. While in Kashmir he studied Buddhist philosophy and became an expert in both the Hinayana and Mahayana intellectual traditions. A climactic moment came when he visited the site of the Buddha's awakening at Bodh Gaya, contemplated the depth of human suffering, and was reduced to tears.

When Xuanzang returned to China, he brought back many manuscripts and was recognized as one of the most learned interpreters of Buddhist philosophy. He became a great favorite in Chinese folk tradition, and the novel *Journey to the West* gives a charming, popular version of his exploits.

CHAPTER TWO

ASPECTS OF THE DIVINE

Whereas many religions focus on the worship of God or other divine beings, Buddhists focus on the figure of the Buddha—a human being who discovered how to bring suffering to an end and escape the cycle of death and rebirth. Buddhists approach the figure of the Buddha with reverence, as others might worship a divine or supernatural being. They also respect the power of local spirits or deities.

The Mahayana set itself apart from earlier traditions by developing a rich array of celestial *buddha*s and *bodhisattva*s who function as supernatural beings to guide believers on the path to salvation. Today it is just as common for a Buddhist to practice the Mahayana by chanting the name of a celestial *buddha* or invoking the compassion of a celestial *bodhisattva* as it is for them to sit alone in meditation.

LEFT: A Nepalese mandala *of 1860 depicting the celestial* buddha Vairochana *("Radiant") in the central circle and four other* buddhas *in the corners of the square. The* mandala *also depicts numerous other sacred beings.*

Theravada Buddhism insists that Siddhartha Gautama was very definitely a human being, who achieved complete *nirvana* (enlightenment; see pp.58–9) and died, never to be reborn. When a Theravada devotee makes an offering to an image of the Buddha, this is not to be understood as an act of divine worship, but a means to gain karmic merit and to be reminded of the Buddha's virtues, which one should always strive to emulate.

This does not mean, however, that Buddhism has nothing resembling the divinities of, for example, ancient Indian tradition. In the Mahayana, those who progress to the highest stages of the path to *buddha*-hood—the *bodhisattva*s ("*buddha*s-to-be," or "future *buddha*s")—are said to accumulate such power from their many works of compassion and wisdom that they are able to act as if they were gods. These extraordinary figures are known as "celestial *bodhisattva*s." They can intervene miraculously in this world, and can even create heavenly realms where people may be reborn into bliss for reasons that depend as much on the compassion of the *bodhisattva*s as on the merit of the individual worshiper. At the end of their careers as *bodhisattva*s they become "celestial *buddha*s" and attain even more remarkable powers. But many *bodhisattva*s postpone *buddha*-hood to assist ordinary devotees on the path to *nirvana*.

The line between a *bodhisattva* and a *buddha* can sometimes be indistinct. According to the Mahayana *Lotus Sutra* (see pp.42–3), the Buddha himself was merely the manifestation of a great *bodhisattva* whose long career has not yet ended. Realizing that people in this world needed an example of a fellow human being who had experienced the process of attaining *nirvana*, he manifested himself as Siddhartha Gautama and went through a show of achieving *parinirvana* (final *nirvana*). But this was not the end of his career: he continues to manifest himself in a compassionate way as long as there are others who need his help.

The concepts of celestial *bodhisattva*s and *buddha*s made it possible for Mahayana Buddhism to develop an elaborate "pantheon" of deities. One of the most important of these many deities is the *bodhisattva* Avalokiteshvara ("Lord Who Looks Down"), who has been called the personification of the compassionate gaze of the Buddha. Avalokiteshvara's compassion is invoked by pronouncing the mantra, *"Om Mani Padme Hum"* ("O Jewel in the Lotus"), which is popular as a meditation mantra. *Om* and *Hum* are untranslatable syllables— *Om* is said to be the sacred sound from which the universe was created and is believed by some to contain the essence of true knowledge.

A 19th-century gilt bronze statuette of the bodhisattva *Maitreya who features prominently in the Mahayana Buddhist traditions of Asia.*

In Indian Buddhism, Avalokiteshvara became associated with a female *bodhisattva* called Tara, who embodied the feminine aspect of his compassion. In China, where Avalokiteshvara is worshiped under the name Guanyin, the *bodhisattva*'s male and female identities became compounded, and Guanyin came to be worshiped mainly in female form. Tibetans feel a special kinship with Avalokiteshvara (whose name in Tibetan is Chenrezig). They claim that he has taken a vow to protect the nation of Tibet and is manifested in the person of every Dalai Lama.

Important celestial *bodhisattva*s also include Maitreya, the *buddha* of the future age, who will be the next *bodhisattva* to enter the world and become a *buddha*. Like Avalokiteshvara, Maitreya is said to rescue people in danger: in China, where he is called Mile Fo, messianic movements have at times proclaimed his imminent arrival and the transformation of society according to Buddhist principles. Other celestial *bod-hisattva*s are Manjushri, the *bodhisattva* of wisdom, and Kshitigarbha, the consoler of the dead and protector of travelers, pilgrims, and children.

The best known celestial *buddha* is Amitabha ("Infi-nite Light"), who is said to have established a paradise, the "Pure Land," on becoming a *buddha* (see pp.90 and 92). Anyone who remembers the name of Amitabha, especially at the moment of death, will be reborn in the Pure Land and come face to face with Amitabha himself. The worship of Amitabha Buddha had great impact in China and Japan, where he is called Amituo Fo and Amida Butsu respectively (*fo* and *butsu* = *buddha*). Indeed, during the social and political turmoil of the Kamakura Period (1185–1333), the worship of Amida became one of the most important elements in Japanese Buddhist life. The Buddhist reformer Honen (1133–1212) made the worship of Amida accessible to people who had no specialized training in Buddhism, and Shinran (1173–1263)—the founder of Japan's Jodo

Shinshu, the "True Pure Land Sect"—insisted that salvation depended only on the grace of Amida rather than on one's own efforts. The traditions founded by Honen and Shinran continue to be the most popular form of Buddhism in Japan and are represented in North America by the Buddhist Churches of America.

Other important celestial *buddha*s include the physician-*buddha* Bhaishajyaguru ("Teacher of Healing") and the "Sun Buddha" Vairochana ("Radiant"), the central *buddha* in many of the *mandala*s, or "sacred circles," of Tantric Buddhism. The *mandala* symbolizes the relationship between the macrocosm and the microcosm: it represents the entirety of the cosmos and also the mind and body of the practitioner. *Mandala*s are used in Tantric ritual and meditation to help the devotee unify his or her vision of the cosmos; to contemplate the integration of the self and the world; and to overcome the distinction between *nirvana* and the realm of death and rebirth.

One of the most common of these sacred images is known as the "*Mandala* of the Five Buddhas" and plays a central role in the Tantric Buddhism of Tibet and in the Shingon tradition of Japan. It takes as its starting point a configuration of five celestial *buddha*s: Vairochana in the center, Amitabha in the west, Amoghasiddhi in the north, Akshobhya in the east, and Ratnasambhava in the south. The *mandala* is expanded and elaborated by a process of symbolic association to include five colors, five personality traits, five wisdoms, and so on, with each element of every pentad associated with one of the five *buddha*s. The *buddha*s are also associated with five goddesses located at the center of the *mandala* and at the four intermediate points of the compass.

As well as appearing at the centre of many *mandala*s, Vairochana, who is identified with the sun, was also important in the acculturation of Buddhism to Japan, where Vairochana was identified with Amaterasu, the sun goddess who heads the Shinto pantheon.

In addition to this host of widely worshiped celestial beings, Buddhism has also always found room for the reverence of local deities and spirits. The Buddha himself is said to have been protected by a *naga* (in Indian tradition, a *naga* is a snake deity that controls the rain; in Buddhism, *naga*s also guard the treasures of the tradition). *Stupa*s (funerary mounds; see pp.66–7) are often associated with *yaksha*s (gods of wealth and good fortune) and *yakshi*s (fertility goddesses). In southeast Asia, Hindu gods such as Indra and Vishnu function as important Buddhist guardian figures, and the faith embraces many local and regional deities in China, Korea, Japan, and Tibet.

The Land of Bliss

66 Then the Blessed One said to Shariputra: 'In the west, Shariputra, many hundreds of thousands of *buddha*-fields from here, there is a *buddha*-field called the Land of Bliss. A perfectly awakened *buddha*, by the name of Infinite Life (Amitayus), dwells in that land and preaches the Dharma. Why do you think it is called the Land of Bliss? In the Land of Bliss no living beings suffer any pain in body or mind, and they have immeasurable reasons for pleasure. . . .

'When any sons or daughters of good family hear the name of the Blessed Tathagata (or Buddha) of Infinite Life and keep it in mind without distraction for one, two, three, four, five, six, or seven nights, then, at the moment of death, the Buddha of Infinite Life will stand before them, leading a group of *bodhisattva*s and surrounded by a crowd of disciples, and those sons or daughters of good family will die with minds secure. After their death, they will be born in the Land of Bliss, the *buddha*-field of the Tathagata of Infinite Life.

'This is what I have in mind, Shariputra, when I say that sons or daughters of good family should respectfully aspire for that *buddha*-field.' 99

From the *Shorter Sukhavativyuha Sutra*, translated by Malcolm David Eckel.

Commentary

The *Shorter Sukhavativyuha Sutra* (Discourse on the Land of Bliss) gives a vivid picture of devotion to Amitabha Buddha (here known as Amitayus, the Buddha of Infinite Life). This *sutra* was composed in India in the early centuries of the Common Era and had immense influence on the practice of Mahayana Buddhism in India and in the Buddhist countries of north and east Asia.

According to the tradition that surrounded this text, a *bodhisattva* named Dharmakara promised long ago that, when he attained awakening and became Amitabha Buddha or Amitayus, he would create a blissful land to save living beings from suffering. This land is depicted as a celestial paradise, full of beautiful trees, lotus ponds, and the sounds of birds proclaiming the virtues of the Buddha. Anyone who recalls the name of Amitabha Buddha is to be reborn in this land and proceed irreversibly to supreme awakening.

The key to salvation in this tradition is the power of Dharmakara's promise or "vow." The vow becomes effective at the moment of his awakening and acts as the grace of the Buddha to lift people to rebirth in the blissful land. When believers "respectfully aspire for this *buddha*-field" they bring their own aspirations into harmony with the vow that created Amitabha's paradise.

CHAPTER THREE

SACRED TEXTS

According to tradition, the Buddha achieved his awakening under the Bodhi Tree in silence, and many Buddhists say that the content of his awakening can never be expressed in words. But this has not prevented the development of a complex and elaborate scriptural tradition to transmit his words to subsequent generations.

Each of the early Schools developed a distinctive body of canonical literature. Of these, only the Pali canon of the Theravada now survives. With the rise of the Mahayana came new scriptural texts and new problems of interpretation. In India, the corpus of authoritative Mahayana literature expanded with relatively few limitations. Today, the Chinese and Tibetan canons provide an enormous treasure trove of Buddhist tradition and an eloquent testimony to the power of the Buddha's awakening.

LEFT: A Buddhist devotee turns a "prayer wheel" in a temple at Kyicho, Bhutan. Each "wheel" is a cylinder containing sacred prayer texts, which are believed to be activated when the cylinder is spun by the worshiper.

After the Buddha's death, his followers are said to have called the First Buddhist Council to recite the content of his teaching (see p.15). The council established a procedure for memorization that allowed the teaching to be transmitted orally for almost five centuries before it was committed to writing. Written versions of the canonical collections exist in all Buddhist cultures and are often treated with great reverence, but the oral tradition is still of central importance. Owing in part to this practice of oral transmission, Buddhism has no single canon of scripture—different schools and traditions regard different collections of texts as authoritative.

While Buddhist canonical literature is variable and new texts have often been added, it is still considered a source of authority, not only because it provides a record of the Buddha's teaching but because it provides access, in a certain sense, to the Buddha himself. Buddhist sacred texts represent the most important, enduring aspects of the Buddha, what Buddhists refer to as his "Dharma Body" (see p.15). A line in the Pali *Samyutta Nikaya* says: "What is there, Vakkali, in seeing this vile body? He who sees the Dhamma [Pali for "Dharma"] sees me; he who sees me sees the Dhamma." The Dharma/Dhamma functions as the continuing presence of the Buddha in the Buddhist community, and is as worthy of respect as the Buddha himself. Buddhist texts are often recited or copied as acts of devotion, and it is not uncommon, especially in the Mahayana tradition, for texts to be placed on altars as objects of worship, alongside, or even instead of, images of the Buddha.

The most conservative canon of Buddhist writings is the *Tipitaka* ("Three Baskets") of the Theravada tradition. Written in Pali, it is often referred to simply as the Pali Canon and contains ancient material from the earliest stages of the oral tradition alongside texts possibly composed in the second century BCE. The *Tipitaka* (Sanskrit, *Tripitaka*) is said to have been written down in 29BCE under King Vattagamani of Sri Lanka.

The three "baskets" are the three sections of the Pali canon: the *Sutta* (Sanskrit, *Sutra*) *Pitaka*, *Vinaya Pitaka*, and *Abhidhamma* (Sanskrit, *Abhidharma*) *Pitaka*. The *Sutta Pitaka* generally consists of the Buddha's doctrinal discourses and ranges from short poems to long prose narratives about the Buddha's previous lives. The *Vinaya Pitaka* is concerned with rules of discipline and includes stories that illustrate Buddhist moral principles. The *Abhidhamma Pitaka* provides a systematic analysis of the categories of Buddhist thought.

The traditional interpretation of the Pali canon owes a great deal to the monk Buddhaghosa, who came to Sri

Lanka from India in the fifth century CE. He collected and translated a large body of Sinhalese commentaries on the Pali texts and his most important work, the *Visuddhimagga* ("Path to Purification"), is an authoritative guide to the practice of Theravada Buddhism.

The development of the Mahayana tradition is intimately connected with the evolution and dissemination of its scriptures. The earliest Mahayana texts can be dated to the first century BCE. Important Mahayana writings were translated into Chinese as early as the second century CE, and texts that came to assume canonical status were produced in India after 1100. India never produced a Mahayana canon that was as clearly fixed as the Pali canon, although informal Mahayana collections existed as early as the second century CE.

The oldest extant catalog of Chinese Buddhist canonical literature dates from 518CE. The first printed version of the Chinese *Tripitaka* (as it is referred to there, using the Sanskrit form of the Pali word *Tipitaka*) was made during 972–983CE, at the beginning of the Song dynasty. The Tibetan canon was collected by the scholar Buton (1290–1364) and was first printed in its entirety in Beijing in the early fifteenth century.

The Chinese and Tibetan canons each give the impression of being a codification of a monastic library.

These 12th-century "Perfection of Wisdom" sutra*s are written on palm leaves which have been threaded together ("thread" is the literal meaning of* sutra*).*

Clearly, for both canons, the concept of "canonicity" was quite loose. There was a core of literature (known in Sanskrit as *sutra* and in Tibetan as *bKa'*) that bore the direct authority of the *buddha*s and *bodhisattva*s. These *sutra* portions of the Chinese and Tibetan canons both include a section called the "Perfection of Wisdom" (Sanskrit, *Prajnaparamita*), which provides some of the most basic accounts of the *bodhisattva* ideal and the concept of "emptiness." Taking a fairly short text as their starting point, the Perfection of Wisdom *sutra*s grew to include as many as one hundred thousand lines and were condensed into brief texts such as the *Diamond* and *Heart* *sutra*s. Around these core *sutra* portions of the Chinese and Tibetan canons accumulated a body of doctrinal, philosophical, and interpretive literature known in Sanskrit as *shastra* and in Tibetan as *ten*, or "teaching."

The most extensive collection of Tantric texts is found in the Tibetan canon. Like other Buddhist canonical literature, it ranges widely in form, from the simple songs of the Indian Tantric saints to elaborate commentaries on Tantric ritual, meditation, and symbolism. The Tibetan tradition generally classifies Tantric texts in four categories: ritual (*kriya*), practice (*charya*), discipline (*yoga*), and highest discipline (*anuttarayoga*). The *Mahavairochana Tantra* ("Tantra of the Great Vairochana"), a text that had central significance in Chinese and Japanese Tantra, belongs to the *charya* category. To the *anuttarayoga* category belong texts such as the *Hevajra Tantra* and *Guhyasamaja Tantra* that focus on the immediate realization of "emptiness." Buddhist Tantric literature in India evolved gradually from the seventh to the twelfth centuries CE.

The *Lotus Sutra* has functioned in East Asia almost as a compendium of Mahayana doctrine and has had wide impact on the religious and philosophical development of the Mahayana tradition. The *sutra* is the source of a famous parable in which the Buddha is represented as a father who lures his children out of a burning house by promising them different "vehicles." When the children get outside, he gives them the "great vehicle" of the Mahayana. The parable points to the relationship between Mahayana teaching and that of the "lesser" vehicles associated with the earlier schools.

The enormous variety of Buddhist scriptures has led to many controversies about scriptural authority and interpretation. Members of the Eighteen Schools (*nikaya*s; see p.16) attacked the Mahayana by claiming that its *sutra*s were not the actual teaching of the Buddha. The Mahayana responded by saying that the teaching of the Schools was merely a preparatory teaching, which the Mahayana superseded. Within the Mahayana, the Madhyamaka School argued that only certain Mahayana texts were definitive in meaning (*nitartha*), while others had a meaning that required interpretation (*neyartha*). The Chinese and Tibetan traditions produced several complex schemes of classification to reconcile contradictions and determine which texts could be relied on for the most definitive teaching. The Tantric tradition dealt with issues of interpretation by insisting that the meaning of the *tantra*s was deliberately veiled and could be correctly interpreted only by a qualified teacher (Sanskrit *guru*; Tibetan *lama*).

The Discourse on Turning the Wheel of the Dharma

66 Thus have I heard. At one time the Lord was staying
in the Deer Park at Isipatana, near Banaras. There the
Lord spoke to a group of five monks: 'O monks, someone who has gone forth into the monastic life should
avoid two extremes. What are the two? One is devotion
to passions and worldly pleasures. This is inferior,
common, ordinary, unworthy, and unprofitable. The
other is devotion to self-mortification. This is painful,
unworthy, and unprofitable. By avoiding these two
extremes, O monks, the Tahatagata has realized the
Middle Path. It gives vision, it gives knowledge, and it
leads to calm, superior insight, awakening, and *nirvana*.

'And what, O monks, is the Middle Path? It is
the Noble Eightfold Path: right views, right thoughts,
right speech, right action, right livelihood, right effort,
right mindfulness, and right concentration. This, O
monks, is the Middle Path realized by the Tathagata.
It gives vision, it gives knowledge, and it leads to calm,
superior insight, awakening, and *nirvana*.' 99

From the *Samyutta Nikaya* LVI.11, translated by Malcolm David Eckel.

Commentary

The Buddhist scriptural tradition traces its origin to the Buddha's first sermon, or the first turning of the wheel of the Dharma. The Pali version of this sermon gives a concise summary of basic Buddhist doctrine, including the Middle Path. Buddhist scripture carries great authority, and prodigious effort has gone into the memorization, copying, transmission, and preservation of the Buddha's words. But it is wrong to equate the authority of the Buddha with any particular formulation of his teaching. The Buddha's teaching has been compared to a raft—when people use a raft to cross a river, they leave the raft behind and go on their way. When someone uses the Dharma to cross the river of suffering, the words of the Dharma can be left behind.

With its practical approach toward the authority of scripture, the Buddhist tradition has been remarkably flexible about developing new scriptures to respond to new cultural situations. The *sutra*s of the Mahayana constituted a "second turning of the wheel of the Dharma" to introduce the *bodhisattva* ideal. The *tantra*s of the Vajrayana introduced another body of scripture to express a new method of awakening. New scriptures have played a role in Chinese Buddhism, and they have often contributed to the vitality of Buddhism in Tibet.

CHAPTER FOUR

SACRED PERSONS

If the goal of Buddhist life is to follow the example of the Buddha, it should be no surprise that the tradition has produced many remarkable figures. During the Buddha's lifetime, several monks and nuns followed in his footsteps and, according to tradition, attained *nirvana* (see p.90). As monastic communities became sophisticated centers of learning and meditation, they continued to play a formative role in the development of the Indian tradition, as well as throughout the rest of Asia.

With the appearance of the Mahayana, the *bodhisattva* ideal meant that it was no longer necessary to be a monk or nun to follow the example of the Buddha. In the Mahayana tradition, there are many who have achieved a special degree of sanctity or authority outside the structure of a monastic community.

LEFT: Tibetan Buddhist nuns participate in a debating session in the courtyard of Dolma Ling nunnery, Dharamsala, India.

To be a "sacred person" in the Buddhist tradition is, above all, to imitate the example of the Buddha. The most basic way to do this is to embark on a monastic life in pursuit of *nirvana* (perfect enlightenment). The greatest exemplars of the monastic ideal were the Buddha's first followers, such as his chief disciple, Shariputra (in Pali, Sariputta). Shortly after his conversion by the Buddha, he became an *arhant*, or "worthy one"—one who, like his master, had attained *nirvana*. Converted at the same time was his friend Maudgalyayana (Pali, Moggallana), who was reputed to possess the magical ability to quell the hostile forces of nature and to travel at will to the highest levels of the cosmos. He became popular in Chinese Buddhist legend as Mulian, who journeyed to Hell to intercede for his mother.

One of the most remarkable of the Buddha's early disciples was Angulimala ("Garland of Fingers") who, before he met the Buddha, is said to have been a mass murderer who wore his victims' fingers as a necklace. However, after meeting the Buddha, he was so moved by his account of the Dharma that he became a monk and eventually attained *nirvana*.

The Indian monasteries of later centuries also produced personalities renowned for their courage, learning, or meditative attainments. The great Chinese monk Xuanzang (596–664CE) visited India in the early part of the seventh century, studied philosophy in the Indian monasteries, and left us an account of scholar-monks who vied for royal patronage in public debate. Among the products of the sophisticated monastic world were the Mahayana philosophers Shantarakshita and Kamalashila, who presided over the foundation of the first Buddhist monastery in Tibet, and Atisha, who helped reintroduce Buddhism to Tibet during the "Later Diffusion."

The roster of monastic figures in east and southeast Asia and Tibet who helped shape the religion is almost inexhaustible. In Sri Lanka, for example, the Indian monk Buddhaghosa (fifth century CE) collected the indigenous commentaries and gave definitive shape to the Theravada tradition in southeast Asia. In China, the monk Huineng (638–713CE) became the Sixth Patriarch and founder of the Southern school of Chan ("Meditation")—his iconoclastic version of Chan eventually became the dominant tradition in China and the source of Japanese Zen.

The Japanese monk Kukai or Kobo Daishi (774–835CE), traveled to China and brought back a form of Chinese Tantric Buddhism that was known in Japan as the Shingon ("True Word") School. He also introduced the phonetic writing system that is used in Japan today to supplement the use of Chinese characters. In the Kamakura period, the monk Dogen (1200–1253) followed Kukai's path to China and brought back a new and vigorous form of meditation to create the Soto school of Zen. In fourteenth-century Tibet, the monk Tsong kha pa (1357–1419) performed an extraordinary feat of intellectual synthesis to produce the Gelukpa tradition and the school of the Dalai Lamas.

The monastic practice of Buddhism continues today with such widely revered figures as Thich Nhat Hanh (1926–), a Vietnamese monk who headed the Buddhist Peace Delegation during the Vietnam War and preaches the Buddhist virtue of "mindfulness" in the West. For many, Buddhists and non-Buddhists alike, perhaps the most visible living example of the "Buddha ideal" is Tenzin Gyatso, the fourteenth Dalai Lama (see p.99).

In the Tantric tradition, especially in Tibet, there has been a complicated interaction between the ideal of the scholar-monk in a monastic community and that of the solitary *siddha* or "saint." The Indian Tantric tradition describes *siddha*s, such as Maitrigupta (or Maitripa), who achieved their meditative breakthroughs on the fringes of civilization, in the forests or cremation grounds, working with unconventional and charismatic teachers.

A Japanese monk collecting alms. The words bhikshu
("monk") and bhikshuni *("nun") come from a Sanskrit
root that means "to beg."*

Padmasambhava, the Indian Tantric saint who shared in the foundation of the first Tibetan monastery, is pictured as a solitary figure with extraordinary powers. His consort, Ye-shes-tsho-gyal, was a powerful figure in her own right.

The Tibetan "saint" Milarepa (1040–1123) worked for many years with the irascible guru Marpa before he was given his initiation and retired into the mountains to live as a solitary *siddha*.

One of the most important institutional developments of the *bodhisattva* ideal was its extension to include a form of sacral kingship, a tradition that has existed in Buddhism since the third century BCE and the time of the emperor Ashoka, who assumed a special status as a Dhamma-raja (Sanskrit, *Dharma-raja*, "Righteous King") for his policy of protecting and promoting the Dharma (see p.16).

As the Mahayana tradition developed, revered Buddhist princes and kings came to be regarded as *bodhisattva*s. Such figures include Prince Shotoku, who played a crucial role in the introduction of Buddhism to Japan, and the Dalai Lamas of Tibet, whom Tibetan Buddhists venerated as the incarnation of the celestial *bodhisattva* Avalokiteshvara. The respect accorded to their status as *bodhisattva*s enabled the Dalai Lamas to assume responsibility for the secular as well as the religious governance of Tibet.

Not all examples of the monastic ideal have been men. During his lifetime, the Buddha agreed to ordain his aunt and create an order of nuns. The Pali canon contains a text, known as the *Therigatha* ("The Eldresses' Verses"), which contains many eloquent songs that have been attributed to this first group of nuns. Today, the lineage of nuns has died out in many Buddhist countries, but there are active female orders in Tibet and China, and movements are afoot to revive orders in other countries.

During the Kamakura Period in Japan, several major movements broke with the monastic ideal and allowed their leaders to be married. This pattern has continued to the present day. The leadership of the Jodo Shinshu ("True Pure Land Sect"), which traces its origin to Shinran, now has a married clergy and does not attempt to abide by the rules of monastic life. The same is true of the Japanese denominations, such as the Soka Gakkai and Rissho Kosei-kai, that trace their origin to the charismatic Japanese reformer Nichiren (1222–81). Nichiren brought a prophetic message to Japan and called upon the nation to return to the true practice of Buddhism.

Milarepa Meets His Teacher

    By the side of the road, a large, corpulent monk with sparkling eyes was plowing a field. As soon as I saw him, I felt inexpressible and inconceivable bliss. For a moment, his appearance stopped me in my tracks. Then I said: 'Sir, I have been told that Marpa the translator, direct disciple of the glorious Naropa, lives in this place. Where is his house?'

    For a long time he looked me up and down. Then he said: 'Where are you from?'

    I said: 'I am a great sinner from upper Tsang. He is so famous that I have come to ask him for the true Dharma.'

    He said: 'I will introduce you to Marpa, but now plow this field.'

    From the ground he pulled some beer that had been hidden under a hat, and he gave it to me. It was good beer, and it tasted great.

    He said, 'plow hard,' and he went away.

From *Mi la ras pa'i rnam thar*, translated by Malcolm David Eckel.

Commentary

There are few more dramatic moments in the story of the Tibetan saint Milarepa (1040–1123) than his first encounter with Marpa, the man who was to become his teacher. Milarepa had studied black magic, and then he practiced it in order to wreak revenge on a group of hostile relatives. Tormented by his crime, he sought out a teacher who could help him escape from the weight of his sin. Marpa accepted the challenge, and put Milarepa through a process of severe punishment and discipline before he gave him the initiation that set him free. Milarepa's humility and his willingness to accept extreme hardship in pursuit of the truth have made him one of Tibet's most beloved saints.

The student-teacher relationship is a crucial part of practice in many Buddhist traditions. Stories of the Buddha often emphasize his "skillful means," by which he perceived the distinctive needs of his disciples and developed a teaching that would be effective for them. For students of Tantric Buddhism, the teacher functions as a representative of the Buddha to guide the student through the dangers of the path. In Chan or Zen Buddhism, the master transmits a lineage of teaching "outside words and letters" that goes back to the Buddha himself.

CHAPTER FIVE

ETHICAL PRINCIPLES

Traditional accounts of Buddhist ethics focus on the "Noble Eightfold Path" that leads from the world of suffering to the achievement of *nirvana*. To follow this path, a person must avoid the evil actions, such as killing and stealing, that lead to negative consequences in this life and the next. A person also has to discipline the mind through meditation and to develop an awareness of the nature of reality.

The practical details of Buddhist ethics have been negotiated differently in different parts of the Buddhist world, particularly in the Mahayana countries where the active ideal of the compassionate *bodhisattva* tended to replace the more contemplative ideal of a solitary seeker of *nirvana*. But Buddhist ethics has never lost its practical concern for the development of the total personality.

LEFT: A 12th-century Chinese painting depicting the Buddha giving alms to the poor—an example of a "good action" that will aid the soul's progress toward the attainment of nirvana.

The spirit of Buddhist ethics is expressed in the story of a man named Malunkyaputta, who tells the Buddha that he will not listen to his teaching until he has answered a series of questions, such as "How was the world created?" and "Will the Buddha exist after death?" The Buddha responds by comparing Malunkyaputta to a man who has been shot by a poisoned arrow but refuses to let it be pulled out until the physician can tell him what the arrow is made of, who shot it, and so on. For Buddhists, all speculation is subject to one practical principle: it is valuable only if it can directly help a person to remove the "arrow of suffering" and find the way to *nirvana*. Any other type of speculation, like Malunkyaputta's questioning, is incidental.

In the Mahayana lands of north and east Asia, the ethical ideal of the *bodhisattva* became the central principle of moral practice for Buddhist monks and nuns as well as laypeople. The *bodhisattva* cultivates the virtues of compassion (*karuna*) and wisdom (*prajna*). These two principles are expressed in the "*bodhisattva* vow": "May I attain *buddha*-hood for the sake of all other beings!"

The virtue of compassion is an active ideal, centered on relieving the suffering of others. This includes helping others to attain *nirvana*, even to the extent of postponing one's own entry into *nirvana* in order to do so.

Wisdom is more contemplative. It focuses on seeing through the "veil of illusion" that clouds ordinary experience, thereby becoming free from suffering oneself.

The basic guide to the attainment of *nirvana* is the "Noble Eightfold Path," a process of discipline with eight components: "right understanding," "right thought," "right speech," "right action," "right livelihood," "right effort," "right mindfulness," and "right concentration." Alternatively, the fundamental prerequisites for *nirvana* can be expressed as three principles: abstention from harmful actions (*shila*, "moral conduct"); a disciplined mind (*samadhi*, "mental concentration"); and a proper understanding of the self and the world (*prajna*, "wisdom").

These principles are related to the traditional Buddhist understanding of the law of *karma*, or moral retribution, that governs the process of death and rebirth. A person should abstain from harmful actions because they will lead to punishment in a future life and thus make it doubly difficult to escape the cycle of death and rebirth. "Mental concentration" helps remove the desire and hatred that lead to harmful actions. And "wisdom" removes the false sense of self that feeds the whole process of desire, hatred, and harmful action.

For Theravada Buddhist laity, and indeed most other

Buddhists, "moral conduct" is summarized in the Five Precepts: no killing, no stealing, no abusive sex, no lying, and no intoxicating beverages. Novice Theravada monks observe five further precepts: no eating after mid-day, no use of ornaments, no attending entertainments or shows, no use of money, and no use of soft beds. However, once fully ordained, monks are bound by more than two hundred rules found in the *Vinaya Pitaka*.

The practice of "mental concentration" (*samadhi*) can take many different forms in the Buddhist tradition. One of the most basic techniques is to sit with a straight back and crossed legs, and cultivate "mindfulness" (Sanskrit *smrti*, Pali *sati*) of one's breathing. The purpose is to calm the mind, diminish harmful emotions, and become more fully aware of the flow of reality that makes up the self and the world. Other forms of meditation involve a deliberate cultivation of mental images, often of *buddha*s or *bodhisattva*s, to serve as the focus of worship.

The cultivation of "wisdom" (*prajna*) also takes many forms. In the Theravada tradition it is associated with the study of the *Abhidhamma*, the third section of the Pali canon, and its key concept is the doctrine of "No-Self." To be wise (or, in the words of the Noble Eightfold Path, to have "right views") is to see that the self changes at every moment and has no permanent identity.

In the Mahayana tradition, the understanding of "No-Self" is expressed in the doctrine of "emptiness." For many practitioners of the Mahayana, all things are seen as "empty" of identity. *Nirvana* is not simply a goal to be sought at the end of a long process of discipline—it can be experienced in the emptiness of the present moment.

A monk sits in contemplation of Buddhist scriptures at the great temple complex of Angkor Thom, Cambodia.

The Foundations of Mindfulness

66 At one time the Lord was staying at Uruvela, under a fig tree on the bank of the Neranjara River, having just become awakened. As the Lord was isolated and secluded, he had the following thought: 'This is the only way for living beings to become pure, to overcome grief and pain, to end suffering and sadness, to attain the right path, and to realize *nirvana*, namely, the four foundations of mindfulness.'

What are these four? A monk should live in such a way that he practices body-contemplation with regard to the body. He should be energetic, attentive, and mindful, and he should restrain ordinary covetousness and discontent. A monk should do the same with regard to the feelings, the mind, and mental states. This is the only way for living beings to become pure, to overcome grief and pain, to end suffering and sadness, to attain the right path, and to realize *nirvana*, namely, the four foundations of mindfulness. 99

From the *Samyutta Nikaya* XLVII.18, translated by Malcolm David Eckel.

Commentary

An essential prerequisite for the attainment of *nirvana* is the facility to calm the mind and allow its passions to cool. In the Mahayana tradition, this "mindfulness" is often viewed as an essential prerequisite for compassion as well: as the mind becomes focused and calm, it is more possible to be attentive to the suffering of others.

Buddhists often begin their meditation with a simple exercise of mindfulness. Sometimes a person practices mindfulness in a formal way by sitting with his or her legs crossed, in a traditional meditative posture, and being attentive to the movement of the breath. But the same form of mindfulness can be extended to every kind of human activity. When one is lying down, one should be aware that one is lying down. When one is sitting, one should be aware that one is sitting. When one is walking, one should be aware that one is walking.

At its most basic level, this practice is meant to cultivate clarity of mind: for one to become aware of the thoughts and feelings that flood the mind in the process of everyday experience. But mindfulness also allows the mind to become calm, just as a lake becomes calm when there is no longer any wind to stir up its waters into waves, or as a fire begins to cool and go out when it is no longer stoked by fuel.

CHAPTER SIX

SACRED SPACE

In the Buddhist tradition, spaces become sacred by their association with the Buddha or with other sacred persons. Historically, the prototype of a Buddhist shrine was a *stupa*, or funerary mound, that contained the relics of the Buddha's cremated remains. *Stupa*s continue to function as important focal points for worship, not only in northern India but across the Buddhist world, as do temples dedicated to the worship of particular *buddha*s or *bodhisattva*s.

As the seat where the Buddha achieved his awakening, the cosmos itself can be considered sacred. The same can be true of particular countries, like Tibet, or particular geographical sites, such as mountains, that are associated with Buddhist deities. Even the seat of a practitioner's meditation, as a replica of the thrones of the *buddha*s, may be viewed as sacred.

LEFT: Master Soen Ozeki raking gravel in the Zen garden at Daisen-in, Kyoto, Japan. The white gravel represents the purity of the mind. The tree represents the Buddha's awakening.

In his final instructions to his disciples, as recorded in the Pali *Mahaparinibbana Sutta*, the Buddha requested that his body should be cremated and the remains enshrined in a series of *stupa*s, or funerary mounds, to serve as focal points for worship and meditation. The basic form of a Buddhist shrine replicates one of these early *stupa*s, with a large central mound surrounded by a railing and topped by a square structure with a central post holding a series of parasols. In the earliest *stupa*s, the relics of the Buddha were housed in the square structure, but later they were enshrined inside the central mound. As the form of the *stupa* evolved in India, the mound came to be decorated with representations of the Buddha, events of his life, or important stories from Buddhist texts. To pay homage to the Buddha at one of these traditional shrines, a worshiper could make offerings in the same way a Hindu devotee might make offerings to an image of a Hindu god, with flowers, candles, incense, and so on; or a person might walk around the *stupa* in an act of ritual circumambulation.

The basic *stupa* was elaborated in many different ways in different lands. In southeast Asia, shrines commonly retain the low, rounded shape of a traditional *stupa*. In Tibet, the structure has been elongated vertically into the shape of a *chorten* or "offering place." In

China, Korea, and Japan, the soaring shape of a pagoda is derived from the graceful parasols that used to adorn the top of *stupa*s in India.

At the great Buddhist temple at Borobudur in Java, the simple path of circumambulation has been elaborated into a series of ascending galleries, decorated with the story of Sudhana, a young Mahayana pilgrim in search of enlightenment. On the top of the structure, the worshiper is confronted by an open platform with an array of individual *stupa*s, each revealing an image of the seated Buddha. In the center of the platform stands a large, vacant *stupa* representing, it seems, the empty clarity of the Buddha's awareness—there are few more elegant and powerful representations of the Buddha's awakening in all of the Buddhist world.

Indian Buddhists established a tradition of temple-building following the Hindu style. The earliest Buddhist temples were created in caves in western India. Typically, the cave entrance led into a large open space where worshipers could sit or stand in front of a small *stupa* or an image of the Buddha. Sometimes the Buddha-image was in a separate room similar to the *garbha-grha* or "womb-house" of a Hindu temple. In recent years, there have been efforts to rebuild some of the important Indian Buddhist temples that were destroyed in the twelfth and thirteenth centuries. For example, a Buddhist organization called the Mahabodhi ("Great Awakening") Society has led the restoration of the temple at Bodh Gaya, on the site where the Buddha achieved his awakening.

Indian Buddhist temple architecture was highly influential throughout the Buddhist world. The Temple of the Tooth in Kandy, Sri Lanka, and the Temple of

The Buddhist temple of Borobudur on the island of Java, Indonesia. This remarkable transformation of the traditional stupa *is a representation of the cosmos in three dimensions.*

the Emerald Buddha in Bangkok, Thailand, are sacred to the royalty of both countries and have served as symbols of royal power. The Jokhang in Lhasa is said to house the oldest image of the Buddha in Tibet and has functioned for centuries as an active center of Buddhist pilgrimage. The great temple at Nara, Japan, played a decisive role in establishing the relationship between Buddhism and the Japanese imperial dynasty.

In the twentieth and twenty-first centuries, Buddhist temples have become common sights in Europe and North America. Los Angeles is sometimes called the most complex and varied Buddhist city in the world, and its many sacred sites include the sprawling Hsi Lai temple complex, established by a thriving Taiwanese Buddhist community.

The holy space created by Buddhist sacred architecture can be understood on a cosmic scale. For example, the central dome of a *stupa* stands for Mount Meru, the Buddhist cosmic mountain that marks the center of the world, and the parasols that rise above the *stupa*'s central axis represent the levels of heaven occupied by different categories of gods in ancient Indian tradition. Above the parasols, in the empty space of the sky, lies the formless realm attained by Buddhist "saints" in the highest levels of meditation, and the "*buddha*-fields"—

the dwelling places of celestial *buddha*s and *bodhisattva*s of Mahayana tradition. Thus, to perform a ritual circumambulation of a *stupa* is not simply to recall and venerate the life of the Buddha, but also to orient oneself firmly at the center of the cosmos.

In Indian tradition, the concept of the sacred center was particularly associated with the throne of the Buddha's awakening, or *bodhimanda*, at Bodh Gaya. According to Indian popular legends, all *buddha*s come to the same throne to achieve their awakening. The stone structure now visible under the Bodhi Tree at Bodh Gaya was said to be the top of a diamond throne extending down to the middle of the earth. The concept of the sacred "seat of enlightenment" can also be applied to sacred mountains, such as Mount Kailasa in Tibet and Mount Wutai in China, which are revered as the thrones of powerful *buddha*s or *bodhisattva*s.

Conversely, the idea of the sacred seat also serves to sanctify the simple space in which the ordinary Buddhist sits to meditate. Devotees of Zen remind themselves that the spot upon which they sit for meditation is the throne of all the *buddha*s of the past and future.

In the Buddhist tradition, the bodily relics and physical images of the Buddha that are venerated in shrines constitute his "Form Body." His teaching, known as his

"Dharma Body," is also the object of veneration, often quite literally. Some of the early Mahayana *sutra*s say that any place where the Dharma is expounded should be treated as a "shrine" (*chaitya*) of the Buddha, and classical Indian writings describe shrines where a copy of a Mahayana scripture is set up with great pomp and ceremony to serve as the focus of worship. Many Indian *stupa*s contained sacred texts in place of the relics of the Buddha. Reverence for the physical scripture is also seen in Tibetan temples, where copies of the Mahayana *sutra*s lie on or around the altars, and in the esteem accorded to the *Lotus Sutra* by the Japanese sects tracing their origins to the social and religious reformer Nichiren.

In India and elsewhere the definition of a Buddhist temple or shrine could be quite fluid, and a place that was sacred on account of its association with the Buddha did not have to be marked by a major architectural monument. Many travelers' tales from ancient India tell of small but unusual features of the landscape that were linked with the life of the Buddha. It was claimed that marks on rocks in a stream near Sarnath had been made by the Buddha's robe as he crossed the stream. A ravine in a town near Shravasti had opened up, it was said, to swallow one of the Buddha's enemies. In many places there has been a lively cult of the Buddha's supposed footprints, most notably perhaps at Adam's Peak in Sri Lanka. According to Theravada tradition, the Buddha used his magical power to fly to Sri Lanka, and left the footprints as a mark of his visit.

For centuries, the sacred sites of the Buddhist tradition have also been the focus of pilgrimage. As indicated by the Chinese story *The Journey to the West*, places in northern India associated with the Buddha's life attracted pilgrims from as far away as China until the destruction of Indian Buddhism made such journeys impossible. Buddhists throughout southeast Asia make pilgrimages to sites sacred in their tradition, including Adam's Peak. Tibetans travel to central Tibet to the holy sites of Lhasa, and they make the grueling journey to the west of the country to circumambulate Mount Kailasa. Other mountains are also regular pilgrimage destinations. Chinese Buddhists make a journey to Mount Putuo on a small island off the coast of Zhejiang Province to pay homage to the *bodhisattva* Guanyin, who is said to reside there, and seek her favor. In Japan, Mount Fuji is venerated by many Buddhist sects.

The history of Japanese Buddhism is rich with the recollections of well-known pilgrims. Some, like the Zen founders Eisai and Dogen, traveled to China to pursue their quest for the Dharma. Others, like the poet

Matsuo Basho (1644–94), lived out their quest for awakening on the roads of Japan.

Buddhist sacred places may even by invisible. The apocalyptic *Kalachakra* ("Wheel of Time") *Tantra*, one of the last Tantric texts to appear in India, tells the story of a mythical kingdom named Shambhala, which lies hidden in the mountains to the north of India and is ruled by a righteous Buddhist king. The text prophesies a time when the forces of evil have conquered the world. Shambhala will then become visible and the righteous king will emerge from his citadel, surrounded by his armies, to defeat the forces of evil and reestablish the rule of the Dharma.

The prophecy of the *Kalachakra* represents a type of messianic speculation that has had important influence at certain stages of Buddhist history. For Tibetans, it serves not just as an image of an ideal Buddhist kingdom but also as an idealized symbolic goal for a *yogi* to attain through the process of meditation.

As the utopia of "Shangri-la," Shambhala has become bound up in the Western imagination with the idea of Tibet itself as an idealized Buddhist paradise, its ancient and sacred way of life preserved for centuries from outside influence by the impregnable mountain barrier of the Himalayas.

Guanyin's Home on Mount Putuo

" With brows of new moon shape

And eyes like two bright stars,

Her jadelike face beams natural joy,

And her ruddy lips seem a flash of red.

Her immaculate vase overflows with nectar from year

to year,

Holding sprigs of weeping willow green from age.

She disperses the eight woes;

She redeems the multitude;

She has great compassion;

Thus she rules on T'ai Mountain,

And lives in the South Sea.

She saves the good, searching for their voices,

Ever heedful and solicitous,

Ever wise and efficacious.

Here orchid heart delights in great bamboos;

Her chaste nature loves the wistaria.

She is merciful ruler of the Potalaka Mountain,

The Living Kuan-yin [Guanyin] from the Cave

of Tidal Sound. **"**

From *The Journey to the West*, Vol 1, translated by Anthony C. Yu. University of Chicago Press: Chicago, 1977, p.185.

Commentary

These lines from *The Journey to the West*, the sixteenth-century novel about the travels of the Chinese monk Xuanzang, show the connection between the *bodhisattva* Guanyin and the pilgrimage site at Mount Putuo, an island off the coast of southern China.

Buddhist sacred geography in China associates three mountains with three major *bodhisattva*s: Mount Wutai in Shanxi province is the home of Wenshu (Sanskrit, Manjushri), the *bodhisattva* of wisdom; Mount Emei in Sichuan is the home of Puxian (Sanskrit, Samantabhadra), the *bodhisattva* of virtuous action; and Mount Putuo in Zhejiang is the home of Guanyin (Sanskrit, Avalokiteshvara), the *bodhisattva* of compassion. Mount Putuo has come to be linked with Potalaka, the island home of Guanyin or Avalokiteshvara in Indian tradition.

One of the founding legends about Mount Putuo tells of a Japanese monk named Egaku who was sailing back home with an image of Guanyin. As his boat neared Mount Putuo, it became stuck. He prayed to Guanyin for help, and the boat was drawn to a cave on the shore known as the Cave of Tidal Sound. There Egaku established a shrine to the Guanyin "who refused to leave." Today, pilgrims come to Mount Putuo from all over China to seek the *bodhisattva*'s blessing.

CHAPTER SEVEN

SACRED TIME

Buddhists mark the movements of the seasons and the stages of human life in many different ways. Some festivals and rituals are tied explicitly to events in the life of the Buddha, the preaching of the Dharma, or the practice of the monastic community, but some of the most important events, such as New Year celebrations and marriage ceremonies, are tied only loosely to Buddhist traditions.

On a larger scale, Buddhists have sometimes been influenced by a theory of historical stages, in which the present is believed to be a "degenerate age" and requires a simpler, more direct approach to the practice of the Dharma. Some Buddhists insist that the distinction between different moments in time is insignificant, and reality can only be experienced by absorption in the sacrality of the present.

LEFT: A Burmese boy has his head shaved prior to entering a monastery for a period of training as a novice monk.

For many Buddhists, the most significant festivals in the course of the year reflect stories about the life of the Buddha. In Sri Lanka and other Theravada countries of southeast Asia, the most important Buddhist holiday is "Buddha's Day," or Visakha Puja, which falls on the day of the full moon in the lunar month of Visakha (April–May). This festival commemorates the birth, enlightenment, and death of the Buddha. Devotees mark the occasion by visiting monasteries, venerating shrines or images of the Buddha, and listening to traditional sermons about his life. Tibetans also celebrate the key events of the Buddha's life, but on separate occasions at different times of the year. Most significant is the festival of the Buddha's conception, or incarnation, on the fifteenth day of the first lunar month, one of a range of events that mark the Tibetan New Year.

Celebrations may also center on personal relics of the Buddha. At Kandy, Sri Lanka, Buddhists turn out in July or August to witness the procession of what is believed to be one of the Buddha's teeth in a great festival that is more than a thousand years old. Faxian, a ninth-century Chinese pilgrim, wrote one of the earliest eyewitness accounts of this ancient celebration.

There are festivals in many Buddhist countries to honor important Buddhist teachings or scriptures.

Theravada devotees celebrate the Buddha's first sermon on the full moon of the eighth lunar month, a date that coincides with the beginning of the monsoon season, when monks go on an annual retreat. In Laos, the story of Prince Vessantara, one of the Buddha's previous incarnations (see illustration, p.12), is celebrated annually. Tibet commemorates the *Kalachakra Tantra* every year (see p.73), and Chinese and Japanese Buddhists have annual festivals in honor of Buddhist *sutra*s, most notably the *Lotus Sutra*.

In Theravada countries, the beginning of the *samgha*, or Buddhist community, is celebrated on the full moon of the third lunar month. Celebrants circumambulate Buddhist shrines and listen to sermons that praise the monks as a source of merit for their lay devotees. Individual countries commemorate the arrival of the monastic community on their own shores, and many monasteries honor the date of their foundation.

In south and southeast Asia, the monastic communities observe the custom of the "rain retreat" during the months of the monsoon (July to October). This custom goes back to the earliest days of Buddhism, when the rains made the roads impassable for wandering monks and they had to settle in monasteries for the duration of the season. For monks, the rain retreat is a time for

focused study and meditation; for laypeople, its conclu-
sion has become a time for lively celebration, when they
join the monks in elaborate processions and make offerings of clothing and other necessities to sustain the
monastic community for the coming year.

*Worshipers in Kandy, Sri Lanka, celebrate during the annual
festival in which the sacred relic of a tooth allegedly belonging
to the Buddha is paraded through the streets.*

One of the most important seasonal celebrations in Buddhist cultures, especially in East Asia, marks the coming of the New Year. In China and Japan the New Year celebration is connected only tangentially with Buddhist themes. The Tibetan New Year celebration includes a reference to some of the miraculous events in the Buddha's life, but its main ritual function is to exorcise the evil influences from the past year in order to bring prosperity and good fortune to the community.

An East Asian festival with more explicit Buddhist content is the Festival of the Dead. Celebrated in Japan in mid-July, the O-bon Festival commemorates the efforts of Maudgalyayana, one of the Buddha's first disciples, to save his deceased mother.

Rites of passage are as important to Buddhists as they are to other religious traditions. Buddhists in Theravada countries observe a series of rituals as a child moves from birth to adulthood. In Myanmar, special childhood rites include a pregnancy ceremony, a birth ceremony, a naming ceremony, an ear-piercing ceremony for girls, and a hair-tying ceremony for boys. Frequently there is little in such ceremonies that owes its origin directly to Buddhism (although Buddhist monks are often present to recite chants or prayers). However, once a boy reaches his early teens, monastic ordination often serves as a rite of passage to symbolize his transition from childhood to adulthood. Once ordained, a youth may spend only long enough in the monastery to learn the rules of monastic practice or how to read and write. However, he may decide to take the necessary vows and become a permanent member. The ordination ritual reenacts the events of the Buddha's own renunciation. The young man has his head shaved, dons monastic robes, and pronounces the phrases that indicate his entry into the order. (In the Mahayana lands, there is less stress on ordination as a coming-of-age ritual. But for the few young men or women who choose the monastic path, it is an equally decisive transition into another way of life.)

The same ambiguity that permeates childhood rites in Theravada countries often pertains to "Buddhist" weddings. The Buddha himself hardly serves as an affirmative model of marriage, since he left his family to become a wandering monk. In southeast Asia, Buddhist monks are often invited to weddings to receive offerings and chant auspicious texts, but the Buddhist element in the ceremonies seems only peripheral. In China, even for Buddhists, the ritual of marriage is traditionally governed by Chinese values of filial piety and respect for ancestors. In Japan, traditional weddings usually take place in a Shinto, rather than Buddhist, context.

However, funerals are a different matter. The Buddha's renunciation of his home and earthly comforts was provoked by a vision of old age, sickness, and death, and the rituals surrounding death are decisively linked to Buddhist values. In China, Korea, and Japan, people turn to Buddhist monks and priests to perform their funerals, and family ties with particular temples are often reinforced by yearly acts of offering and remembrance in honor of the deceased. In southeast Asia, funerals frequently last for several days and involve offerings and the chanting of *sutra*s. These are intended to bestow extra merit on the deceased for their benefit in the next life.

Buddhist views of sacred time are not limited to the movements of a single season or to the events of a single life. There is also a Buddhist tradition that relates to the decline of the Dharma from a golden age, that which existed during the life of the Buddha, to a degenerate age in which it is difficult to practice the Dharma in a traditional way. This concept had a profound influence on Japanese Buddhism during the Kamakura Period (1192–1333). Finally, it is important to recognize that for many Buddhists, distinctions in time are unimportant and awakening can occur at any moment.

The Degenerate Age of the Dharma

" The Lord Shakya proclaimed to all celestial beings
that when, in the fifth five hundred years after his
death, all the truths should be shrouded in darkness,
the Bodhisattva of Superb Action should be commissioned to save the most wicked of men who were
degrading the truth, curing the hopeless lepers by the
mysterious medicine of the adoration of the Lotus of
the Perfect Truth. Can this proclamation be a false-
hood? If this promise be not in vain, how can the rulers
of the people of Japan remain in safety, who, being
plunged in the whirlpool of strife and malice, have
rebuked, reviled, struck, and banished the messengers
of the Tathagata and his followers commissioned by
Buddha to propagate the Lotus of Truth?

People will say that it is a curse; yet those who propagate the Lotus of Truth are indeed the parents of all
men living in Japan. . . . I, Nichiren, am the master and
lord of the sovereign, as well as of the Buddhists of other
schools. Notwithstanding this, the rulers and the people
treat us maliciously. . . . Therefore, also, the Mongols are
coming to chastise them. . . . It is decreed that all the
inhabitants of Japan shall suffer from the invaders. **"**

From "Nichiren's Account of the Degenerate Age of the Dharma" cited in Wm. Theodore de Bary, ed., *Sources of Japanese Tradition*. Columbia University Press: New York, 1958, pp.225–26.

Commentary

In common with the first few generations of many religions, early Buddhists had a sense that life was better when the founder of their tradition was still alive. From this idea grew a theory about the decline of the Dharma: for the first five hundred years after the Buddha's *parinirvana* it was possible to practice the true Dharma (*saddharma*); for the next five hundred years it was possible to have access only to a shadow of the true Dharma. In the "last days" (Chinese *mo-fa*, Japanese *mappo*), even this shadowy Dharma had begun to disappear.

This model of historical decline had significant influence on Buddhist practice in India, China, and Tibet, but its most striking impact came during the Kamakura Period (1192–1333) in Japan. There was social turmoil; the country was plagued by incessant warfare; and a Mongol invasion fleet threatened imminent catastrophe. Shinran and Nichiren, a pair of remarkable reformers, preached that the degenerate times called for a fundamental reorientation of Buddhist practice. For Shinran the solution was to trust in the saving grave of Amida Buddha; for Nichiren it was to rely on the power of the *Lotus Sutra*. Both reformers challenged prevailing religious authorities and spawned mass movements that changed the face of Buddhism in Japan.

CHAPTER EIGHT

DEATH AND THE AFTERLIFE

According to the traditional account of the Buddha's life, Siddhartha Gautama, the young man who was to become the Buddha, visited a park outside his palace. In this park, he saw three sights which confronted him with the problem of death: a sick man, an old man, and a corpse. On a later trip outside the palace, he encountered a wandering ascetic who had renounced ordinary life to escape the cycle of death and rebirth. These "Four Sights" inspired Siddhartha to follow the path of renunciation.

Like the Buddha, Buddhists share a keen awareness of death, and cultivate strategies to deal with its challenge—from the moral and spiritual disciplines that insure a favorable rebirth to the meditation and study that allow a person to be released from *samsara*, the endless cycle of death and rebirth.

LEFT: A Tibetan thangka (devotional painting) of the "Wheel of Life," which depicts the human cycle of death and rebirth. There are six realms of rebirth, and it is a person's actions in previous lives that determine which one he or she will enter.

Traditional Buddhist ideas about death are based on the ancient Indian doctrine of *samsara*, variously translated as "reincarnation," "transmigration," or simply "rebirth," but literally meaning "wandering"—from one lifetime to another. By the time of the Buddha, Indian religion had come to assume that life is cyclical: a person is born, grows old, dies, and is then reborn in another body to begin the process again. Rebirth can occur as a human being, deity, ghost, or animal; or else a person may be reborn to punishment in Hell.

The nature of an individual's reincarnation depends on *karma* or moral "action." Someone who accumulates merit or good *karma* in the course of a life will be reborn in a more favorable situation in a future life, perhaps even as a god. The reverse applies to those who perform bad actions. Before they can be reincarnated in a different form, the worst offenders have to eradicate their demerits by suffering in one of the layers of Hell, which are ranked according to the severity of their punishments. The lowest and worst level is reserved for people who have killed their parents or teacher. Just as the inhabitants of Hell can wipe out their sins and be reborn as humans once more, those who rise to divinity can exhaust their merit and slip back into the human realm. No matter how high a person rises on the scale of reincarnation, there is always a danger of slipping back down. No state of reincarnation is permanent.

Traditionally, people endeavor to avoid evil deeds and accumulate merit through acts of worship or donations to monks, in the hope of receiving a better birth in the next life. But Siddhartha Gautama saw *samsara* as an eternal grind of deaths and potential suffering and set out to break the cycle. According to Buddhist tradition, the moment of Siddhartha's "awakening" was under the tree at Bodh Gaya. After he had overcome the temptations of Mara, he entered a state of concentration and resolved that he would not get up until he had attained release from the cycle of death and rebirth.

The first of his insights was the knowledge of his previous births. This was followed by the knowledge of the births of others, and finally by the knowledge of the "Four Noble Truths": the "truth of suffering," the "truth of the origin of suffering," the "truth of the cessation of suffering," and the "truth of the Path." This can be explained as follows. The Buddha's "awakening" began with the realization that all life is filled with suffering, in particular the suffering that comes from seeing a beloved person, object, or experience pass away, as it inevitably must. He perceived that the origin of suffering lies in desire, and that desire comes from a misconception about the nature of things, in particular the nature of the self. By removing this ignorance, Siddhartha was able to bring suffering to an end in the experience that Buddhists call *nirvana*—a word which means literally to "blow out" the fire of ignorance and desire, states which the Buddha perceived to be the "fuel" of *samsara* and the source of suffering.

The Buddha achieved *nirvana* in two stages. At the moment of his "awakening", he realized that he was no longer fueling *samsara* by performing karmic actions— in other words, all desire in him had ceased. Decades later, at the moment of his death, known as his *parinirvana* or "final (or 'complete') *nirvana*," all the Buddha's residual *karma* was exhausted and he was completely released from *samsara*, never to be reincarnated.

Monks and nuns have attempted to follow the Buddha's example and achieve the same liberation from rebirth by renouncing their own attachment to the pleasures and responsibilities of lay life and practicing meditation and good moral conduct. For all Buddhists, the way to *nirvana* involves following precepts such as the "Noble Eightfold Path" (see p.59).

The tradition of Pure Land Buddhism, a form of Mahayana Buddhism that is found principally in China, Japan, and Tibet, holds that if a believer chants with

A 17th-century Japanese hanging scroll that depicts Amida Butsu (Amitabha, top left) surrounded by the faithful.

faith the name of the celestial *buddha* Amitabha (Chinese, Amituo; Japanese, Amida), the latter will visit the believer at the moment of death and convey him or her to rebirth in Sukhavati, the heavenly "Pure Land," or "Western Paradise." Here, free from earthly distractions, the devotee can prepare for *nirvana*, which is guaranteed to all who attain the Pure Land.

The practice of Pure Land Buddhism, or Amidism, has its roots in the ancient Indian idea that meditation on a particular deity at the moment of death will help ensure rebirth in that deity's celestial domain. Amidism continues to dominate the understanding of death in some of the most popular forms of Japanese Buddhism, particularly in the Jodoshu ("Pure Land School") and Jodo Shinshu ("True Pure Land School") movements in Japan and in the Buddhist Churches of America.

In Japanese Zen Buddhism, there is a tradition of composing a poem at the moment of death. These poems often give powerful expression to the sense of detachment that infuses the story of the Buddha's own *parinirvana*. One Zen warrior, who was forced to commit suicide out of loyalty to his feudal lord, wrote of death as a sharp-edged sword that cut through the void, and compared it to a cool wind blowing in a raging fire. It was as if his own sword were the sword of the Buddha's wisdom that cut through the illusions of life and blew out the fire of existence.

Buddhist funerals are intended to assist the deceased into a better birth. Tibetan funerals go a step further, aiming to ensure the person's liberation from *samsara*. The Tibetan *Book of the Dead* is one of the best-known Buddhist funeral texts. Over a period of as long as forty-nine days—said to be the length of time it takes for a person to be reborn in another life—a *lama* chants the words of the text, at first in the presence of the corpse and later before a picture of the deceased.

The text describes an array of benevolent and wrathful *buddha*s who will appear to the deceased in the "intermediate realm" (*bar-do*) between death and rebirth, and explains that a person should recognize these forms as nothing but manifestations of his or her own mind. According to the text, it is possible for the deceased to unite with these forms and thereby be liberated from the cycle of death and rebirth. For those who are not successful in uniting with the *buddha* forms, the *Book of the Dead* goes on to explain how to achieve a positive incarnation in the next life. This practice seems to be directed as much at the living as the dead—it helps mourners to come to terms gradually with their loss, and to prepare themselves for their own transition out of this life.

Japanese Poems on the Moment of Death

66 The sharp-edged sword, unsheathed,
Cuts through the void—
Within the raging fire
A cool wind blows. **99**   By Shiaku Sho'on

66 Throughout the frosty night
I lay awake. When morning bells
rang out, my heart grew clear—
upon this fleeting dream-world
dawn is waking. **99**   By Hasegawa Shume

66 On a journey, ill:
my dream goes wandering
over withered fields. **99**   By Matsuo Basho

66 Mt. Fuji's melting snow
is the ink
with which I sign
my life's scroll,
'Yours sincerely.' **99**   By Kashiku

From *Japanese Death Poems*, compiled by Yoel Hoffmann. Charles E. Tuttle, Co.: Boston 1986, pp.51, 67, 85, 82.

Commentary

The religious traditions of ancient India put special emphasis on composing the mind at the moment of death, for that was the moment that prepared the way for rebirth in another life. Also, it was the moment when the personality or soul could become free from the rebirth altogether. The same emphasis is reflected in the Japanese tradition of writing poems when close to death.

The Japanese often make eloquent use of Buddhist images that express the fleeting, dreamlike, and sorrowful quality of experience in this world. They also reflect a longing for the incisive insight that will cut through the suffering of life and lead to an experience of detachment and peace. However, many Zen poets and practitioners insisted that it is misleading to focus solely on the moment of death—in their view, because every aspect of life is impermanent, there is no moment that does not share in the experience of death.

When the poet Matsuo Basho lay on his deathbed and his pupils hinted that he should leave them a death poem, he said that any of his poems could be considered a meditation on death. His response reflected the insight of the Zen master Dogen, who said: "Each moment is all being, is the entire world. Reflect now whether any world or any being is left out of the present moment."

CHAPTER NINE

SOCIETY AND RELIGION

The Buddhist community, or *samgha*, has four divisions: monks, nuns, laymen, and laywomen. The monks and nuns renounce the duties of ordinary lay people and live lives of simplicity. The laity marry, have families, grow crops, accumulate and distribute wealth, maintain order, and do everything to enable the inhabitants of the monasteries to pursue *nirvana*.

However, the simple divisions of Buddhist society are made more complex by the different roles that exist within the monastic community —by the complexity of occupations and functions within the lay community, and by the shifting relationships that bind the two orders of society, monastic and lay, together. In recent years, Buddhist communities have expressed Buddhist social teachings in new ways in order to respond to the challenge of modernity.

LEFT: His Holiness Tenzin Gyatso (1935–), the 14th Dalai Lama. Largely due to his influence, Tibetan Buddhism is one of the most prominent Buddhist cultures in the world today.

The Buddhist monastic community began as a group of wanderers who followed the Buddha through the towns and villages of northern India. As time went on, the monks and nuns adopted a more settled lifestyle. During the months of July and August, the monsoon rains forced them to stay in a fixed location. Out of this practice grew the institution of the monastery (*vihara*), which in time became the central institution in Buddhist life. Supported by the patronage of kings and wealthy donors, the great Indian monasteries became centers of learning, not just in Buddhist philosophy and ritual, but in secular arts such as literature, medicine, and astrology. Buddhist lands in southeast Asia in particular developed sophisticated monastic traditions that often were closely linked to royal power.

The tradition of Buddhist kingship looks back to Ashoka, a ruler of the Maurya empire in northern India in the third century BCE (see p.16), as the ideal *dharmaraja* or "righteous king." Ashoka converted to Buddhism after a particularly bloody military campaign and he attempted to promote a policy of *dharmavijaya*, "righteous conquest" by means of the Dharma rather than by force of arms. Buddhist monarchs have traditionally viewed themselves as "righteous rulers" in the style of Ashoka and have protected the monasteries in their domains in return for monastic recognition of their own legitimacy as rulers.

The most unusual variant of the institution of Buddhist kingship occurred in Tibet, where the "Great Fifth" Dalai Lama took advantage of the weakness of his rivals to become the country's full secular *and* religious leader. Tibet was governed by this distinctive combination of monastic and secular leadership for centuries until 1950, when the newly founded People's Republic of China invaded the country to enforce its claims to hegemony. The fourteenth Dalai Lama, Tenzin Gyatso, a youth of fifteen, remained in office but was forced to acknowledge Chinese overlordship.

In 1959 an uprising against Chinese rule provoked harsh intervention and the Dalai Lama fled to India. From this time, the Tibetan monasteries suffered severe persecution and many were destroyed, especially during the Cultural Revolution (1966–76). However, in the 1980s, controls on religious activities were relaxed and monastic life began again in some of its traditional centers. From exile in India, the Dalai Lama has continued to call for peaceful efforts to preserve Tibet's culture and autonomy. He was awarded the Nobel Peace Prize in 1989. But China has been unreceptive to his appeals and seeks to control Tibetan religious affairs.

*Aung San Suu Kyi (1945–) reads a statement at the gate of
her home, to which she has been mainly confined by the Burmese
military because of her pro-democracy activities.*

Buddhists around the world, while respecting the large and socially influential monasteries, also retain a reverence for the individual "saint" who retires in solitude or with a small group of companions to seek *nirvana* away from the affairs of society. The forest-saints of Sri Lanka or Thailand are often treated as the great heroes of the tradition and provide an important counterweight to, and critique of, life in the major monasteries and society as a whole. When Dogen, the founder of the Soto Zen sect in Japan, rejected the requests of an imperial envoy to involve himself in the life of the Japanese court, and threw the envoy out of his monastery, he was enacting an ancient Buddhist ideal of withdrawal from the affairs of state.

The relationship between monks and ordinary laypeople is best seen in the ancient practice of the morning begging round, still observed in southeast Asia. Each day, monks leave the monastery and go from house to house to beg their food for that day. This simple ritual ties the monks and laity together in a network of mutual support. The monks receive the alms that aid their quest for *nirvana*, and laypeople are offered a daily opportunity to practice generosity and thereby accumulate merit that will lead them to a better rebirth in the next life. This reflects the broader idea of "interdependent causation" taught by the Buddha. According to this, every person has a distinct role to play in the framework of Buddhist society, but all are bound together in a network of mutual dependence.

In the nineteenth and twentieth centuries, the traditional structures of Buddhist society in southeast Asia have been shaken by the challenges of European colonialism, secularism, Communism, and modern science. Under the influence of the modernist and scientific vision of Buddhism developed by the Theosophical Society, the Sri Lankan monk Anagarika Dharmapala (1864–1933) led an important movement to rationalize Buddhist practice, strip away "superstitious" aspects, and mobilize the Buddhist community in a struggle against British colonial rule. Since Sri Lanka (as Ceylon) gained independence in 1948, Buddhist institutions have flourished there, but not without struggle. Ethnic violence between Buddhist Sinhalese and Hindu Tamils has introduced an element of religious conflict into Sri Lankan society that seems difficult to reconcile with the image of Buddhist tolerance and peacefulness.

Myanmar is particularly notable for its distinctive vision of the active relationship between Buddhism and politics. After independence (as Burma) from Britain in 1948, the first prime minister, U Nu (1907–95), promulgated a program of reform referred to as "Buddhist Socialism." U Nu said that a true socialist state should promote equality, discourage acquisitive instincts, and provide enough leisure so that the people may devote time to meditation and the pursuit of *nirvana*. Ousted by the military in 1962, U Nu lived in exile in India for a number of years before returning to Myanmar in 1980 and becoming a Buddhist monk.

In other parts of southeast Asia, Buddhists have faced the challenge of living under secularizing Communist regimes. In Vietnam, for example, Buddhist institutions have remained fairly active, but in Cambodia they suffered massively from the devastation wrought nationally by the Khmer Rouge government of 1975–79 and are still recovering.

The twentieth century also saw an attempt to revive Buddhism in its homeland of India as part of a critique of the traditional caste system. Dr. Bhimrao Ramji Ambedkar (1891–1956), an "Untouchable" from the Indian state of Maharashtra, saw in Buddhism an ideal of equality and social justice that could relieve the oppression of the disadvantaged castes in Indian society. He created an important social movement based on Buddhist principles that continues to play a role in Indian religious life and politics.

A Spiritual Revolution

“ The quintessential revolution is that of the spirit, born
of an intellectual conviction of a need for change in
those mental attitudes and values which shape the
course of a nation's development. A revolution which
aims merely at changing official policies and institutions with a view to improvement in material condi-
tions has little chance of genuine success. Without a
revolution of the spirit, the forces which produce the
iniquities of the old order would continue to be
operative. . . . It is not enough merely to call for
freedom, democracy and human rights. There has to
be a united determination . . . to make sacrifices in
the name of enduring truths, to resist the corrupting
influence of desire, ill will, ignorance, and fear.

Saints, it has been said, are the sinners who keep on
trying. So free men are the oppressed who go on trying
and who in the process make themselves fit to bear the
responsibilities . . . which will maintain a free society
. . . . A people who would build a nation in which
strong, democratic institutions are firmly established
as a guarantee against state-induced power must first
learn to liberate their own minds from apathy and fear. ”

From *Freedom From Fear and Other Writings* by Aung San Suu Kyi. Penguin: London, 1991, p.183.

Commentary

In July 1988, the Burmese ruler General Ne Win, head
of the Myanmar Socialist Programme Party, held a
national referendum on the country's political future.
Popular opposition to authoritarian military rule
crystallized around the figure of Aung San Suu Kyi, who
has become one of the most celebrated examples of a person who brings Buddhist religious values to bear on secular affairs. Her father, Aung San, was a colleague of
U Nu and had led the movement for national independence until his assassination in 1947.

Aung San Suu Kyi's political writings, gathered in
a collection called *Freedom From Fear*, speak eloquently
about a modern quest for democracy and human rights,
about the traditional Buddhist values of truth, fearless-
ness, and loving kindness, and about the connection
between spiritual and political forms of liberation. In
recognition of her campaign for peaceful democratic
reforms, she was awarded the Nobel Peace Prize in 1991.

As Aung San Suu Kyi's career demonstrates, it is
possible for women to play an important role in the
political life of the modern Buddhist countries of
southeast Asia. But it cannot be denied that traditional
ideas of male dominance are still deeply rooted in the
culture of this and other regions.

GLOSSARY

arhant a "worthy one," someone who has attained *nirvana*, has cut ties with *samsara*, and will never be reborn.

bodhisattva Sanskrit, "future *buddha*," "*buddha*-to-be" (literally "awakening being"). In Buddhism, an individual who attains awakening (*bodhi*) but opts to defer *nirvana* (see below) in order to assist others in their spiritual quests, thus epitomizing the ideal of the Buddhist path according to the Mahayana tradition.

buddha Sanskrit, "awakened one." In Buddhism, one who has attained awakening and *nirvana* (see below) by his own means. There have been many *buddha*s—the most recent of which was Siddhartha Gautama—and there will be many more *buddha*s to come. Used as a title ("the Buddha"), the term refers to Siddhartha, the founder of Buddhism.

Chan Chinese *chan* (Japanese *zen*), "meditation," from the Sanskrit *dhyana*. A school of Chinese Buddhism in which the pursuit of enlightenment centers on the practice of meditation.

dharma Sanskrit, "truth," "order," "righteousness," "duty," "justice." The term is used in both Hinduism and Buddhism; as a proper noun ("the Dharma"), it refers to the "truth" about human existence discovered and taught by the Buddha.

karma Sanskrit, "action." The balance of merit and demerit accumulated by an individual, which determines the nature of one's next reincarnation.

mandala a meditational device that is a representation of the Buddhist universe.

mantra a powerful word or phrase that is spoken or chanted in ritual or as an aid when practising meditation.

nirvana Sanskrit, literally "blowing out." In Buddhism, a state free of all ignorance and desire, in which one ceases to accumulate *karma* (see above) and thus achieves liberation from the cycle of death and rebirth.

samsara the beginningless cycle of death and rebirth from which beings strive to gain liberation.

Tantra the name given to ancient sacred texts and the movements to which they were foundational in Buddhism (from ca. 7th century CE). These texts stress ritual, symbolism, and rapid enlightenment involving the concept of "wrathful deities." *Mandala*s (see above) commonly appear in the Tantra.

Zen Japanese *zen*, "meditation," from Chinese *chan* (see above). A school of Japanese Buddhism that focuses on meditation.

Pure Land Sukhavati, the "Western Paradise" where the *buddha* Amitabha reigns.

GENERAL BIBLIOGRAPHY

Aung San Suu Kyi. *Freedom From Fear and Other Writings.* rev. ed. New York: Viking, 1991.

Bechert, Heinz and Gombrich, R., eds. *The World of Buddhism: Buddhist Monks and Nuns in Society and Culture.* New York: Facts on File, 1984.

Conze, Edward, ed. *Buddhist Scriptures.* New York: Penguin, 1959.

Eckel, Malcolm David. *To See the Buddha: A Philosopher's Quest for the Meaning of Emptiness.* Princeton: Princeton University Press, 1994.

Gombrich, R. and Obeyesekere, G. *Buddhism Transformed: Religious Change in Sri Lanka.* Princeton: Princeton University Press, 1988.

Gombrich, R.F. *How Buddhism Began: The Conditioned Genesis of the Early Teachings.* London: Athlone, 1997.

Horner, I.B. *Women Under Primitive Buddhism: Laywomen and Almswomen.* London, 1930; repr. Delhi: Motilal Banarsidass, 1975.

Kitagawa, Joseph M. *Religion in Japanese History.* New York: Columbia University Press, 1966.

Lamotte, Etienne. *History of Indian Buddhism from the Origins to the Saka Era.* Translated by Sara Webb-Boin. Louvain-la-Neuve: Institut Orientaliste, 1988.

Nakamura, Hajime. *Indian Buddhism: A Survey With Bibliographical Notes.* Delhi: Motilal Banarsidass, 1987.

Rahula, Walpola. *What the Buddha Taught.* New York: Grove, 1974.

Snellgrove, David and Richardson, Hugh. *A Cultural History of Tibet.* Boulder, CO: Prajna Press, 1980.

Suzuki, Daisetz T. *Zen and Japanese Culture.* Princeton: Princeton University Press, 1959.

Tambiah, S.J. *Buddhism Betrayed? Religion, Politics, and Violence in Sri Lanka.* Chicago: University of Chicago Press, 1992.

Tambiah, S.J. *World Conqueror and World Renouncer: A Study of Buddhism and Polity in Thailand against a Historical Background.* Cambridge: Cambridge University Press, 1976.

Tenzin Gyatso, the fourteenth Dalai Lama. *Freedom in Exile: The Autobiography of the Dalai Lama.* New York: HarperCollins, 1990.

Trainor, Kevin, ed. *Buddhism: The Illustrated Guide.* London: Duncan Baird Publishers, 2001.

Tweed, Thomas A. *The American Encounter with Buddhism, 1844–1912: Victorian Culture and the Limits of Dissent.* Bloomington: Indiana University Press, 1992.

Williams, Paul. *Mahayana Buddhism: The Doctrinal Foundations.* London: Routledge, 1989.

Wright, Arthur F. *Buddhism in Chinese History.* Stanford: Stanford University Press, 1959.

Zwalf, W., ed. *Buddhism: Art and Faith.* London: British Museum, 1985.

INDEX

Page numbers in **bold** refer to major references; page numbers in *italics* refer to captions

ACKNOWLEDGMENTS AND PICTURE CREDITS

Unless cited otherwise here, text extracts are out of copyright or the product of the author's own translation. The following sources have kindly given their permission.

Origins and Historical Development, p.24: from *The Life of Hiuen-tsiang*. Translated by Samuel Beal. Kegan, Paul, Trench, Trübner & Co. Ltd: London, 1911, p.105.

Sacred Texts, p.44: from the *Samyutta Nikaya* LVI.11, edited by M. Leon Feer. Pali Text Society: London, 1898. Translated by Malcolm David Eckel.

Sacred Persons, p.54: from *Mi la ras pa'i rnam thar* (*texte tibétain de la vie de Milarepa*), edited by J.W. de Jong. Mouton & Co.: Dordrecht, 1959, p. 55. Translated by Malcolm David Eckel.

Ethical Principles, p.62: from the *Samyutta Nikaya* XLVII.18, edited by M. Leon Feer. Pali Text Society: London, 1898. Translated by Malcolm David Eckel.

Sacred Space, p.74: from *The Journey to the West*, Vol 1, translated by Anthony C. Yu. University of Chicago Press: Chicago, 1977, p.185.

Sacred Time, p.84: from *Sources of Japanese Tradition*, edited by Wm. Theodore de Bary. Columbia University Press: New York, 1958, p.225–26.

Death and the Afterlife, p.94: from *Japanese Death Poems*, compiled by Yoel Hoffmann. Charles E. Tuttle: New York, 1986, pp.51, 67, 85, 82.

Society and Religion, p.104: from *Freedom From Fear and Other Writings* by Aung San Suu Kyi. Penguin: London, 1991, p.183.

The publisher would like to thank the following people, museums, and photographic libraries for permission to reproduce their material. Every care has been taken to trace copyright holders. However, if we have omitted anyone we apologize, and will, if informed, make corrections in any future edition. **Page 2** Graham Harrison, Oxfordshire; 7 British Library, London; 12 British Library, London; 18 Graham Harrison, Oxfordshire; 26 Art Archive, London/Musée Guimet Paris/Dagli Orti; 30 British Museum, London; 36 Hutchison Library, London/Sarah Errington; 41 British Museum, London; 46 Corbis/Alison Wright; 51 Hutchison Library, London/Liba Taylor; 56 Art Archive, London/Museum of Fine Arts, Boston; 61 Corbis Stockmarket; 64 Magnum Photos, London/Rene Burri; 68 Magnum Photos, London/Bruno Barbey; 76 Magnum Photos, London/Bruno Barbey; 80 Panos Pictures, London/D. Sansoni; 86 DBP Archive; 91 British Museum, London; 96 Panos Pictures, London/Neil Cooper; 100 Panos Pictures, London/Alison Wright.